Being
and
Possibility

Being
and
Possibility

Robb Thomson

Being and Possiblility
Copyright ©2017 Robb Thomson

ISBN 978-0-692-86881-2
Published by Robb Thomson LLC
robb@cybermesa.com

Cover design by Eric Thomson

Interior design by Robb Thomson
Font: Bembo

Special thanks to my daughter, Judy Thomson for her encouragement and insightful line by line editing. Christopher Johnson has coached my progress as a poet and edited the final product. Thanks also to Candace Walsh as a thoughtful editor of all my poetry.

Thanks, finally, to Eric Thomson for his artful design of the cover.

Contents

Introit

The Steeple   1

I

Dwelling in Truth   3
Silence   4
Joy   5
Daybreak   6
Day to Day   7
Prayer   8
Song out of Sight   9
The Turn   10
Pluck   11
My Shoes   12
The Raven and the Egg   14
Ode to a Cloud   16
Our River in Summer   18
Song of Songs   20
Who?   21
Two Women at a Water Fall   22

II

Earliest Memoory   25
A Soul's Prayer   26
The Lincoln   28
My Way   30
Bosoms   32

My Lap   34
Singing Sky   36
A Certain Stream   37
Sea Monsters   38
We   40
On the Bed   42
Ending   43

III

Model Change   46
Life to Be   48
Dangerous Times   50
Our Jobs are Gone!   51
Chaos   52
Donkeys   53
November 6 2016   54
Dug In   55
My Crowd   56
Turning   57
In the Age of Trump   58
We Like Walls   60
The Beautiful People   62
After the Flood   64
Two-year-old   68

IV

A Future Mound   72
Alone   74
Origins   77

Giants in the Earth 78

Perfection 80

Meaning 81

Mess 82

V

A Cosmic Mind 85

Soon? 86

Present at the Creation 88

Bots 90

VI

Enchanted Worlds 93

Becoming 96

I and Thou 98

In the Genes 99

The Drums 100

Molecular Bonding 102

Knowing You 104

Me & You, Inc. 106

Remembering You 108

To Have Been 110

Coda

Flower, Ne'er the Less 113

Introit

The Steeple

It stands white
above the New England town
and points to the future
its builders knew to lie
beyond the blue.

Generations sat crowded
into family pews below,
and each soul extended
through the spire as neurons
relaying life to the town spirit
hovering above.

Few of the townspeople are
descendants of the steeple carpenters,
but the speech they use
was mouthed by them,
and current ways see
ancient origins.

The whiteness
still polarizes the sky
and anchors the diaphanous
spirit that, looking
down, gently pulls
later awareness into ancient orbits.

I

DWELLING IN TRUTH

What I would know surely,
I must know poetically.

Silence

Beneath the silence between words
lies an undersound —
earthy and fecund;

though one word
is history for the next, it is only
from silence the final chord voices.

JOY

Embraced in
joyous dance
under a sceptered sun,

from listless void,
we bid love arise,
immaculate.

DAYBREAK

As the dawn cracks,
spilling its yolk,
a song erupts
to herald the burgeoning day.

DAY TO DAY

How to live well
glitters untouchably
from the blue,

while below knitted brows
my fingers
stretch towards it.

PRAYER

When I have learned to love
more perfectly,
When I have made
more perfect beauty,
When I know more deeply
the meaning of the stars,

Then will I know
a more perfect being.

Song out of Sight

Hating the formless
turbulence of our days,
I long to sing the song
that lies within.

THE TURN

The discord
of human insanity
stirred by daylight's heat

is rendered a gentler mien
by the cooling hush
of evening's caress.

PLUCK

We are fools
to grump over our fate,

when guts
are mostly grit

My Shoes

You're the least of me,
and you'd best not cause a blister
or into the garbage with you.

The Raven and the Egg

My friend liked to play with ravens.
So one day, he took a small egg,
placed it on a rock in full view
of a raven in the vicinity,
then drew a complete circle around it
by scraping his heel in the sand.

Next, we drew back to see the fun.

Our feathered friend immediately saw the egg,
and flew down just outside the circle
to peer at it. He must have
believed the humans had laid a trap
with that circle, and after inspecting
its closure, flew off to a nearby tree
to consider.

He was clearly in agony,
spewing guttural murmurings
while he fidgeted from branch to limb
with his eye always on the encircled egg.

Flying down, he again inspected the circle.
Tentatively, he pecked at it
and jumped back to see what would happen.
Seeing nothing, he again made a tentative peck
and jumped back.

Again, seeing nothing, he became frantic
and hopped around the circle flapping
his wings, till the circle was erased.

Finally, his path to the egg clear,
and his human tormentors defanged,
he grabbed it and flew off.

ODE TO A CLOUD

Fickle one!
You gather
your clan to tower
with menace

over a thirsty land,
while all in it
cower,
watching and waiting,

hoping for a drink
but fearing a drowning,
hoping for rivulets
but fearing a flood.

This is when
the arroyos,
who look as changeless
as moon features

waken with a start
and break out of their banks
to wear new wrinkles

into an old landscape
and wipe out impudent
human intrusions
on dried up flood plains.

But give me all your wanton
wildness —
A merciless sun
has desiccated all life

and turned our skin
into shriveled leather.
I'll catch every drop
I can in my eager mouth

and dam the sweating earth
into catchments of remembrance
for when you roar off
into the horizon's timeless empty.

Our River in Summer

A dense green shades the water
as it falls, fountain-like,
over the rocks emplaced
by a grateful city
for the comfort of the river —
itself created by
manipulating the outlet gates
of a man-made lake
trapped in an upland valley.

Though man-handled,
the river owns itself,
and nourishes a slim strip
of wild through the city center,
unperturbed by the racket.

I belong to its delicate ecology,
though nourished in a different way
from the trees and shrubs
growing natively along its banks.

Not chemical,
my nourishment comes
in the form of a couch
in my self's center where I sit
immersed in the river's song
whose beauty is matched
to the resonance
of my heart.

And when I rise from that lunch,
my day continues to sing
with river song
till time for another sitting.

SONG OF SONGS
A slightly bent Villanelle

O life, tell me Sing!
when the day is gloom —
let death delay his sting.

Show him, who sings
only fated doom,
that life beckons still. So sing!

I walk my river's songing
through summer's bloom:
For her, no death will sting.

And hills that ring
me round, sound a lively blue
and living, surely sing

a song that centuries fling
from here to timbuktu
with nary death nor sting.

So mount and stream, wing
me to a land of eternal womb
where life bids me sing
through death's forbidden sting.

Who?

Who is the delightful person
who just sat next to me
with her joyous nature sparking
the air around us?

How did she find her sunny self
in the infinite possibilities before her,
and fix it in her nature?
And how can I learn that heavenly
fixing from her?

Two Women at a Water Fall

Like a scene from Titian,
two women sat on the rocks
at a small fall in a creek
painting the turbulent stream
as it flowed away sheltered
by the tender Spring foliage
on trees along the bank.

As I mused, the scene shifted
in my mind, and I became aware
of how time would change it —
the women would go home,
the water would go to the Rio Grande,
and the trees would cycle through
the season.

Would time and change destroy
this beauty,
or was the spirit
of that moment stored away
in some far blueness?

Whether or no, that moment
became an ethereal constant
of my life,
for something lay waiting
in my psyche for it to materialize.

I could feel the inner shaking
as it resonated
with my central self,
somehow strengthened it,
and allowed me to become
a newer me.

II

EARLIEST MEMORY

Toddling up the walk
to my new home,
an urgency propelled me to
explore
the beckoning bricks
rising at the end of the walk,
where the mystery of my future
would unfold.

A Soul's Prayer

In the silence
between heartbeats
my soul looks back into itself,

listening for the pregnant sound
of the first toy truck
pushed over that long ago carpet,

and the futures being forged
from my own personal
time machine.

Now those futures
have materialized,
and I sit arranging them

into patterns and parades
that satisfy my late quest
for form.

But the form is elusive
till I open the curtain
drawn close about

to the constellations
that glory beyond.

Robb Thomson

Then, in humility,
I pray a tiny offering
will heighten their holy beauty.

THE LINCOLN

nuzzled the curb while I gaped
at its magnificent engine
through slits in the side
of its intimidating hood.

The chauffeur described
the feel of whispering down the street
at the wheel of this latter-day dragon
while nodding to the wide-eyed
peasants along the route.

There was nothing
in my young depression-rent life
to compare with the power radiating
from this green monster,
and it seemed to hint at how
I might chauffeur my own destiny.

For I saw magic
in the glowing aura
of the physical car
and felt the sweaty spirits forged
into its polished skin
by the hands of its builders.

But the design faults hidden by
that impudent green polish
would make their presence felt
only with hard driving
over my future of
storm damaged roads.

My Way

My first toy was a truck,
and I experienced the great power
that flowed back and forth
through my guiding hand.
I absorbed the workings,
of our Model T, as I helped
my Dad dismantle it in the street;
and from there,
built a scooter
from broken skates
and reveled in the rush of air
past my ears as I careened down
the hill faster than I could run,

all in preparation for tinkering
that malleable
and only partly inanimate world
to my own ends.
You and I have become
masters at that,
and how wonderfully
and, sometimes,
how tragically
have we succeeded.

★★★★

But the awesomeness
of the night sky also imprinted
my mind as beauty incarnate —

its full splendor
was encapsulated even
in the smallest insect,

and ensnared occasionally
in the laborious creations
of human artistry and imagination.

It is to touch ultimacy
when I capture a wisp
in my tinkering

and know my
version of its joy.

★★★★

And as those two joys
seize me in thrall,

I wonder,

do they
also transcend me?

Bosoms

When the cacophony of the day
is too much, nerve must be plucked
from wherever it can be found,
in thin air or deep recess.

No priest can help,
nor the learnèd,
because love comes not
from lecture or rule.

A familiar bosom,
when one can be found,
is all that's needed,
for its been nourished

by communal genes
from primeval times
designed to
moor lonely souls.

My Lap

Lying in the lap of myself,
a thin eye peers
from another world
and seems to want in.

He is a stranger —
I can't reach my hand to him
through an impermeable skin.

Stubborn, though,
he remains fixed in my sight
just beyond reach.

He claims I can only be complete
if he joins me here,
or I join him there,

in a refrain I have heard
from every prophet's lips
since time began.

It is a dance I am asked
to learn, to a music
I am asked to make,
with drums I must learn to beat,

in which we fuse
in the passionate heat
of ecstatic dance.

For when the music stops
and Eros wilts,
I am heaven-restored.

SINGING SKY

The slicing cold of winter
has lost its edge,
the sun is more confident
in a singing sky.

But the tilt Nature designed in the sky
to herald the seasons
brings a load of pollen to my elm
and an ache to my head.

I turn up the volume
in clogged ears
to catch the beat
and shout my own muted joy.

Robb Thomson

A Certain Stream

Like my hand in a mountain stream
flowing moments of being,
I am led deep into the mysteries
of myself where words
lose their way.

There, like a Buddha,
sits my essential self —
a kind of mother
of all I am and can ever be.

But no idle worship is there,
only the joy and peace
of communion,

and the soft flow of being
on the banks of that verdant run.

SEA MONSTERS

Like a living time machine,
the bestiality of the last century
and its mortal threats
still live to haunt my psyche.

I was just out of childhood
when the world I came into
fell brutally apart.

The oceans my forebears
had relied on for protection
were now full of sea monsters
unrelated to the cod we ate with relish.

It was not just a white shark
we could avoid by getting
out of the water —
these monsters were amphibian.

And it was no dream —
the tsunami that swept over
the Europe from which
most of our ancestors came was real,

and when the fleet
we were so proud of
was destroyed in one swipe
of a monster's claw,

a pillow over the head
had no effect —
we were stripped naked.

But we had a toughness
we didn't know about,
and leaders who knew how
to convert possibility into reality.

It came almost as a surprise
when the deadly struggle
agonizingly turned in our favor.

I now know that sea monsters
do exist in depths of the human
oceans we know nothing about,

and that the dice with which we play
aren't loaded in our favor.

WE

sat on the grass at the edge
of a grove of trees and looked out
to a landscape of beckoning mountains
we had not yet climbed,
and the view drew us
into our dream.

There the hills and valleys
were embodied equations,
which fitted the land
like a blanket over a template,
and the whole glowed with
unnatural beauty.

For we were imagining
our lives together where the truth
in our heads would conquer the landscape
stretching before us, because we knew
God was a mathematician.

The vision was as real
as the love we felt for one another,
and two became fused
into the same dream.

Though the image struck deep in her,
it began to bleach under the harsh
light of a realer world,
and the glories of the dream
faded into illusion.

Now, too alone, she stumbled into
the wilds of regular people
bereft of her guiding daemons,
and I, too, was left alone in that other
world to make of it what I could,

while our love was remade
to a different mold.

On the Bed

Mouth open and eyes closed,
you are too still to be alive,
but too present to be gone.

The years are still in a face
that no longer smiles,

as you become
the blue silence of far hillsides.

Ending

Just sit tight a bit longer soul,
while I tie up a gift or two,
and then we'll turn together
for the amen.

III

Model Change

Shock over, it is clear
we are in a struggle
to define who we are.

Polarities thrust
their masked faces at us
from every quarter,

and our days hop
from scene to scene
like bad drama.

But the work of
making meaning for a people
is culture defining,

and grounding myth
for our psyches
is the result.

Boy George
and his hatchet can be
edited,

and my character
suffers or strengthens
in the retelling.

So what is the shining
city on a hill
to become —

a fortress protected
by poisoned moat,
or a statue of liberty, regilt?

LIFE TO BE

What is the future like?

In the midst of WWII, the outcome
was more than scary,
and if it were different than it was,
how many futures
could there have been?

I have spent a life
of future-making
and still don't know
what difference it made
in the larger truth.

But here I sit
on a turbulent ocean
of possibility and try to
envision where oceanic storms
will take those on my
chain of connection.

If the future is the path
of a chaotic Nature
punctuated by human choice,
and if the longer impact
of human choice is never certain,
what can I pass to those coming after?

I will commend a faith in themselves
and point to how a collective will
has brought us out of the stone age
to whatever we are now —
and challenge them with
a future still to be shaped
by their emergent will.

DANGEROUS TIMES

The loss of a job
and becoming
irrelevant

first numbs and puzzles,
but rage at manhood's
theft is not far behind.

No one cares who
the thief was,
so long as there is a scapegoat,

and someone to rouse
the mob to a frenzy.

But I just want a job.

OUR JOBS ARE GONE!

Everyone knows
God provided us
with an inexhaustible earth
to supply our human need —
oil to fuel cars and planes,
gas for central heating,
and coal to burn for light
and TV.

Our grandfathers spent their
lives learning how to find it,
how to dig it out,
and then develop
the dazzling technology
for the standard of living
God made possible.

Now some fools in Washington
are trying to turn it all off,
and we'll be damned if
they will!

We have lost our jobs!

Someone must be getting
paid off —
who?

CHAOS

They say love
is the law of the universe,
but in which universe
does it rule?

Not this one, where
self-interest towers over the land,
and the starkest aggression
is rewarded by the greatest power.

Our people fracture,
knowing only few work
for the common good,
and children
are abandoned to fend
for themselves
in streets ruled by chaos.

Where is that lovely universe
where a bruised cheek
is turned again,
and kindness grows like a flower
to the song of the earth?

DONKEYS

Graceless and brutish,
we are in the year of the donkey,
braying our pain,
yet begging for healing affection.

November 8 2016

Half in shock and half in ecstasy --
that is the schizoid nation we are.
After a night hammering a new
memory structure into our brains,
the morning is the start of a new run
in the knotted thread of time.

What is to be is in fog;
what is dreaded shreds
the self image of half a tribe.
For the past has died
a deeper death than usual,
and the new reality
is an orphan
with parents unknown.

Though they be
diminished and torn,
we will need a whole people
on that day when a better reality
is born, and realer
leaders can grow.

Dug In

We crouch in a storm cellar
while a political hurricane
thunders across the landscape,
leveling much of what we value.
Our hope but a flickering candle
sheltered in cupped hands,
we pull ourselves together
to emerge again.

Even if the ravaging storm
passes in the night, what enormities
will face human will and strength,
and how difficult will it be
to build a shared home
that nourishes everyone?

MY CROWD?

When the great populist
backlash took place, I wondered
what People I was a part of.

Suddenly, I was immersed in a crowd
shoving its way past me into a place
I feared and abhorred.

Attack dogs slashed
their way through decades
of delicate compromise and social change,

making it necessary
to do so much over again,
and do it better.

It will take willingness to fail and fail again
to turn technological change
into social justice and public good,

and repair the damage done
done to our nourishing planet

"How long?"
rings my heart.

TURNING

We are in a turning,
when the world pauses
to take a deep breath
before plunging into the unknown.

The post-war synthesis has frazzled,
and breakneck technology
has cut away old
ways of relating to one another,
even of making a living.

Our dominion over the earth
is confirmed, as brutishness
tears apart the subtle bonds
wrought over eons by slower
and surer kinds of life.

Suddenly we face ourselves
and wonder who we are,
and what we think we are doing.

Like artists painting an Abstract
in fits and starts, we are guided
merely by a scrappy feeling
for loving wholeness,

and our canvas is bare.

IN THE AGE OF TRUMP

Too many of the dear people
I called "friend"
voted crazy last November —
some psychic defect seemed
hidden under their skins.

But when I steal a look again
into those faces I knew so well,
their laughing eyes,
their joyful nature,
their readiness to love
still grins back.

But now there is a no-man's land
between us, where talk is
carefully proscribed
and cheerful openness can suddenly
become anger and hate.

When I meet a new person,
I must proceed with care
till I know where they put their "x"
on the ballot of that awful election.

The easy, many faceted, give and take
between friends can now only
take place on one side
of the line running through
that dreadful mark.

I hate this thing
that makes aliens out of friends
and poisons collective actions
for our common good.

But mainly,
I miss those friends I once had,
whose fascinating quirks
so delighted me,
and wonder what I must do
to turn their charms my way
again?

WE LIKE WALLS

There are the walls of sand
we build at the beach,
there were the walls of Jericho,
the Great Wall of China,
Hadrian's wall,
Stalin's wall,
and now we have Trump's wall.

Shall we wall off the moon?

The Beautiful People

They glow
in the dark like nonstop
fireflies, the light of
their sureness soothing
the pain and doubt of
every thus bless'd neighbor.

They know that days are somber,
not draped with bunting,
but that being alive
is the highest gift
bestowed by the universe.

And they know that being alive
means to love.

They know love
is the antidote for hurt
(even the loss of one most dear),
when new life sprouts
with a flower's glory
from the enduring beauty
of simply loving and being loved.

I capture every spark
I can from them
and carefully nurture
the embers I keep ready
in my heart for when
I can light my own dark.

After the Flood

The climate tsunami
bearing down on us
seems about to tear
the living planet apart.

Who knows how that flood
will alter the ground beneath,
and what it will look like
when its wrath recedes —
for it will recede, even if human kind
is reduced to clutching
a few polar islands for sustenance.

What human geology has brought
this disaster upon us,
and what gods can we call on
for help?

★★★★★

Ours was a difficult birth
with death in the swish
of every blade of tall grass,
and nakedness our lot.
Like jackals,
we became tribal,
with our weapon
a hand-made spear

instead of nature-made teeth.
But as we concocted
better spears
no animal could face
our fury.

★★★★★

As tribes became cities
and cities became cultures,
an enemy's roar now
came from another city
across a mountain or river,
instead of a vicious cat.

But in all our new wealth,
we couldn't forget our origins,
and Daddy Protector
became General Alexander.

And President Trump
waited in the wings.

★★★★★

But hold,

something else was going on —
beauty lovingly made and cherished,
the something that happens
when two hearts become one,
or when brothers and sisters join hands
and dance in a singing air —
even when we sink into
the embracing spirit
of awesome nature.

If other animals live in that ambience
we don't know it.
But we do,
and that is the true center of it.

★★★★★

After the flood,
hauntingly foretold in myth,
we pray that in the eons to come
whatever in our nature has brought
it upon us will be totally wiped
from our psyches,
and that we will be free to develop
the full potential of what remains —

maybe a nature geared
for a long future
to some far dawn when
an emergent humanity
will have a heart strong enough
to take on transforming
a cold and senseless world.

Two-year-old

She searched my face
with the sharp eyes
of a two-year-old — taking nothing
for granted, as she stashed me
into that slot of her erupting mind
where her humanity
was being organized.

Her mother was all she should be,
attentive, but with a loose tether,
supported by a loving father.
Grandfather, overseeing it all,
was sure she was gifted.

But as I delighted in her innocence,
a dark aura surrounded her
like the background of a Rembrandt,
which never touched the light
of her face, but shivered me.

What dreads await this girl?
Will she have the strength to turn
the chaos being prepared for her?
What kind of warning should I voice —
will the love surrounding her
make enough difference?

IV

A FUTURE MOUND

There is a mound
in some far future
covering a city
I know.

Silent streets
follow the archeologist's
furrows overlain
by memory's map.

There are traces of a river,
once carefully tended,
running through the town
but now long dry.

The archeologist
works to find hints
to fit into
a vast pageant

of an old civilization
now extinct
and only dimly remembered
in ancient artifact and myth—
for no one understands
why it died.

The archeologist struggles
to see deeper into the puzzle,
and seems to sense the blackness
I see clearly on my horizon.

ALONE

The vast Empty
enfolds us and all other life,
even as we are mothered
by the warmth of a star
at just the right distance
to nurture an effulgent chemistry
on a condensed fragment of space.

Tethered by the tender bonds
of our families,
we are frightened to our cores to find
an end of family at
the edge of our earth —
and the loneliness
beyond is overwhelming.

We can make up stories
about a larger family
with a loving parent
at its head,
who makes human meanings
to set against nature's chaos.

And my psyche shouts hosanna
to the glory that then
colors the black Alone with
a vast togetherness and purpose
in a friendly starred heaven,
unutterably beautiful
to my astonished eyes.

But it is black space that stares
back when the echoes die.
Then, our eyes shielded
from the starry myth, we look
nakedly at the vastness
that crowds in on us at night.

Dare we imagine bare truth?
Won't the Empty overwhelm us
and fill our souls with its void?

★★★★

But my soul is not a receptacle
for emptiness.
It boils over with spirit
like the empty space that forever creates
virtual particles, hating
its emptiness as it bubbles
froth in a boiling firmament.

75

And in that froth, rising
from the bottom, is my joy
at simply being.

Could it be that the void
hungers for what you and I have,
and that, whatever life is,
its function is to fill the void
and not the other way round?

ORIGINS

The question
from where we come
resounds in every people and time.

Those tales in Genesis,
Hesiod and the Upanishads,
all sing about how our central natures
derive from the structure
of a sensate universe.

But the tale we get from science
about the big bang and evolution
is silent about purposeful natures,
and is limited to simple observations
of how we started living in tribes.

What kind of Ur-myth can be made
from that?
Are meaning and purpose
what We make them to be —
something new in the universe
that only humans can fashion?

GIANTS IN THE EARTH

We were created in a tangled soup
of love and hate
stirred by a careless Nature
from the mud
of a forming planet.

But in moments
of startlement, we snatch
fragments and intimations
of what humanity
promises,

which we breathe into being
slowly and haltingly
over eons of turbulent time
interrupted
by nightmare and brutality.

We have had to do it ourselves,
uncertainly,
with everything new, and mistakes
perceived only in the messes
they engender.

Thus have we stumbled from war
to sonata, from loutishness
to sublimity,
and often do not know
the difference.

Still, we
peer beyond the black zero
of our beginnings
to squint with stinging curiosity
at those hinted possibilities.

PERFECTION

"Perfect" was a word coined
before the mathematicians
properly termed it "infinity."

In the delirium at the end of endurance
when She seems almost touchable,
we seem merely teased
by a mirage of possibility
in the far beyond.

So where is the perfect love,
the perfect beauty, or perfect knowing,
but in running the Way?

Robb Thomson

MEANING?

When the beauties of nature or man
cannot penetrate the cataracts
of eyes grown cynical
from the damage of
an over-indulgent self,
the whole world turns gray.

But soft in the Below,
as in a placid lake,
shy feelings swarm near the surface
ready to be plucked
to quiet the noise
of a rampant body
with joyful play.

Diaphanous and illusive,
they are the ultimate origins of meaning —
themselves but a transparent ghost.
They seep into the intellect
with their silken voices
to become the unplanned
and self-made sinews
of a loving being.

MESS

Nature or God,
it makes no difference which,
threw me and my outsized ego
into a barnyard full
of others just like me
and bade me cope.

The trouble is,
none of us can stand
to be around another for long.

I could try to beat up everyone,
and rule the entire roost alone,
but there're too many tougher than me.

The bees seem to have an answer,
but I'm not a clone,
and there's no queen bee here.

History is full of prophets and saints
who preach empathy and compassion,
but also full of murder on all scales
up to wiping out whole peoples.

Some say the species slowly makes progress,
but it is hard to see,
and I don't have time
for mankind to sort that out for me.

So what do I do?
Who shall I be?

A Cosmic Mind

Some have said
the only way to populate
the universe is to send an armored
robot out there in our place.

A proxy so artfully made
as to love as well as think,
one able to reproduce
when it gets old and tired --

a self contained replica
distilling the wisdom
of the entire race.

But before we send such a stand-in
wandering into space
to propagate a geologically
youthful breed,

have we yet the awareness
nature yearns for?

Soon?

My friend's story is about a planet
taken over by robots.
It tickles our fancies to imagine
how powerful computers
may one day become,
and unsettles us to think
that they could one day replace us.

★★★★

There are two kinds of ultimate limits
for computers:

They are limited by quantum mechanics,
the laws of entropy and general relativity.
Estimates are that these physical limits of computers are
a factor of maybe 10(^20)
beyond current supercomputers.

Logical limits also exist, resulting from
a mathematical theorem by Godel,
that make it impossible to tell
in all cases whether a computer will
present its answer in a finite time.

But within those limits
a vast world exists for computer evolution
into artificial intelligence.

★★★★

So can we ever create
an artificial human offspring
from all that?

Even if one day we could conceive
a way to do it
and the brain to go with it,
we are stumped by the problem of how
a subjective self can arise
from the physicality of any
kind of brain.

So fiction authors, dream on,
we are safe
for now.

Present at the Creation

I remember Illiac,
the already fabled machine
down the street
that pointed to the future.

So, at first shyly,
I visited her, and punched holes
into teletype tape to engage her
with my numerical fancies.

And while waiting, peeked behind
the partition where,
like a great beached whale,
she glowed in her stacks of vacuum tubes.

A surgeon's tap into her memory,
the cathode ray tube in the front room
displayed a raster of dots
upon which she played a sonata,
as my instructions surged
through her brain.

It was as if I could see her masticate my tape,
digest it, and then metabolize it into the knowledge
she then communicated to me.

She made teasing mistakes,
and could never be trusted,
which only added to her allure.
If I could do a computation
on my trusty Marchant in a week,
I didn't bother with her idiosyncracies.

But all that faded as I ultimately found it
impossible to get by without her,
and a marriage of convenience was arranged
lasting through her many progeny.
Mystery now gone, and routine established,
she and her family have moved in permanently.

BOTS!

You and your kind
from the computer cloud
have immigrated into my world
so suddenly that my welcome mat
has been trampled and muddied
beyond washing.

You try to relieve
wants I hadn't noticed
and tell my doctor about
ills I didn't know I had.

You fill my days with unwanted efficiency
like the broom of the sorcerer's apprentice,
and my spontaneous rhythms
turn into jolting urgencies.

Such a flurry and racket
can be fun except
you keep it up all night,
so I can neither sleep nor think.

So, now, fellows,
this is enough,
and it is time for me
to get on with normality,
while you go about your
own affairs.

But I should have guessed —
you are here to stay,
any resemblance to my old norm
is going fast,
and I am as dizzy from it all
as clothes in a dryer.

But look here,
you ingrates,
you are our creatures,
and if, like Jaweh, we must have
a flood, perhaps we can also
have a following rainbow.

VI

Enchanted Worlds

I

When I sink into myself
I often find more than one person:

There is the friendly one
who invites me
to talk over my troubles,
or nudges me when a poem
is about to emerge,

and sometimes a quieter one,
who prefers to share silence,
brother to brother,

stretching with me
toward the great "I"
in a shamanic attempt
to penetrate the veil
between the world of the real
and the glowing world that's felt —
and we wander in its gallery
of private enchantment.

II

Like the hushed rustle of leaves,
I sense the presence of you.

Sparks fly across
the divide between us,
lighting fires deep within,
with kindling waiting there
to be ignited.
Our worlds welded by spiritual fires,
we dance in joyous riot
through now open doors.

But if the doors are scorched
and scarred by hot gases
of anger and hatred,
the way to sacred spaces
is barred in distrust.

Then fed by devils
not aroused before,
the fire consumes without mercy,
and chokes both worlds in smoke
while bonds between selves
become chains of slavery.

III

It is a dangerous risk
to open those doors —
but our nature demands it,
and the trick is to know
how to tend the fires.

BECOMING

Buber says social relationship
is the central fact about me.
But how can he be right
when a deeper biology makes sure
I take care of myself,
and stay away from snakes
and cliff edges?

It is the tension between
our dual natures
that drives my day
with first one
and then the other ascendant.

When I am permitted full access
to someone I love, my heart rings
in a harmony not thinkable
in any solo voice.
Another universe opens,
not of things, but of being.

It's then I revert to my deepest self —
where Totality roots me
in its vast beauty,
and I know its need to embed
even me within its All.

Those are the bequests of biology,
and each is a treasure that includes
in a mysterious way the other.
I'll never make a unity of them —
they are united only in the me
that actuates in each moment.

I and Thou

Since I am Me,
I know you must be You,

but to know You happens
only when I break through Me
and you through You
in a love beyond either.

But so much of You
lies in mystery
and challenge —

can I know more than one You
at once,
and can I find a magnified,
or only a diluted loving
if I do?

Robb Thomson

IN THE GENES

The gravity that grips galaxies
and solar systems and the molecular
forces that bind atoms
are everywhere in a delicate dance

with the fiery energy
that first exploded
the primordial atom
and still fuels the stars —

a dance that foretells
the future of mankind
where love of self
fights care for others
in every heart.

But just as the sun clasps
a wayward earth
and warms it
against the cold of space,

so does our affection
and devotion bind a choleric
and turbulent race, as it flashes,
comet like,
through mindless time.

THE DRUMS

It was a hand clapping frenzy
with drums and a wild music
uniting the primal sound
of a roomful of singers,
the whole driven as by the beat
of a single great heart.

It was a fleeting thing —
as the sound died,
we looked at each other
in wonder at the way our separateness
opened for those moments
into an intimate communion
of shared being.

★★★★★

We first know ourselves
as helpless children, our souls open
like the mouths of newly hatched starlings,
when we're nourished
soul to soul in total nakedness
deep in the nests built for us
by parents.

But in time, lessons in self protection
are also passed,
and fence making begins.
Fortunately
our fences are semi-porous,
and secret passages are left open
to those few we love
in completeness.

That is, until we are captured
by those drums,
the fences crash,
and we're back, naked
in our first natures.

Then, again, community
becomes a pulsing reality
and we affirm
what we can truly be
to one another.

Molecular Bonding

When two atoms join
to make a molecule, the atoms
lose some of their separateness
and something new is born.

Some of the electrons are shared
so they no longer belong
to one atom or the other,
and now a twosome exists
where there were
merely two ones.

We seem like that
when we discover
our ability to bond with one another,
and break the skins separating us,
to dance together inside a single
skin.

Like the atoms,
a part of our separate spirits
join into a single whole
and our humanity is born.

But nothing like
our dance of delight takes
place for the poor molecule.
Nothing like the glory
that lights our souls in union,
or the thrill
of touching another.

Nothing like the gratitude
we feel for someone simply being there
to receive the love that overflows
our self regard.

KNOWING YOU

You, known deep,
can only be taken slowly
and one at a time
because of the far depths
I must wander in finding you.

When I turn
to taking in
bunches of you at once,
the system only clogs.

But my biology has already
thought of that,
and made me loyal
to my tribe — and tribes come
in many types and sizes.

Tribes are new inventions
in the biological world,
and squabble all the time,
with too little supervision by
the mother tribe of us all.

So let's have a recall,
and do it right.

Surely it is possible
to love all of you at once.

ME & YOU, INC.

My days are filled
with forging a balance
between me and you.

Selfless saints are mythic heroes,
but without knowing myself
how can I fully know you?

If there is no place for you
already embedded in my heart,
then self-regard
is a river in rampage
and my humanity drowns.

For you and I
must be nurtured
with equal compassion,
that we may become
lovingly entwined.

★★★★★

It is when you become many
that I am overwhelmed,
for each of you is a full
vessel.

In the name of the millions
beyond my ken,
we have tried kings and republics
and invented courts for justice,
but the system is rickety,
and tending it
takes unending labor.

At the end of the day,
I know you are there,
and only together could we
have made our private joy.
Yet, it is only in our millions
that a new kind of life comes to be —
firing the whole universe
if we can keep it lit.

Remembering You

In a dream,
I lived again
my complete immersion
in you as we envisioned
the future we would live
together.

No physicality separated us,
as we each looked into the
soul of the other through
the eyes of the universe,
and saw each
completed in the other.

Like a newborn,
we were a flower from the far deep
opening for the first time
to its gloried world.

The word love
is too hackneyed to convey
the state of absolute humanity
we experienced,
and experience again
now and then,

but it is enough to know
final truth is
the warmth of the you
I embrace
in all the dimensions of touch.

It tells me even when
I can only look but not touch,
or even when the other is
too far away to touch,
they are still
touchable.

It is akin to the falling away
of separateness in the presence
of some kind of you
in the vastness of the stars
or an intimate mountain brook.

Thus, my lonely self
is not my most precious gift,
but rather
that I can invite inside
what I find outside,

for the pregnant union
I find there.

To Have Been

In the tender dawn,
only unstated demands;
no Way visible
but to grope in
a mud-fog sucking at feet
and mind.

Getting lost seems the point of it,
till we cover the walls of emptiness
with a furry cloak,
and nurture a slow warmth
in an ember snagged
from hell.

In the end,
'round to a Tender,
remade.

Coda

FLOWER,
NE'ER THE LESS

... The invisible worm
that flies in the night ...
has found out thy bed
of crimson joy ...

From The Sick Rose by Wm. Blake

★★★

In its harnessed beauty,
God's fulfillment;

in its tiny seed,
a universe's power;

though shriveled
by nature's callous wrath,

yet still in all tomorrows,
a flower.

Robb Thomson

ABOUT THE AUTHOR

Robb Thomson grew up in El Paso, Texas during the mid 20's to early 40's of the last century. He was educated at the Universities of Chicago and Syracuse, and spent a career teaching and doing research in physics and materials physics.

In retirement, he now lives in Santa Fe, NM and writes poetry, because, as he dug into the nature of his own being he found it was at bottom a poem.

He has written five earlier books of poems, *Arranging the Constellations*, published by Mercury Heartlink, and *Centering the Pieces*, *O Damn!*, *Wde Places in the Mind*, and *Smiling Deep*, all published by Robb Thomson.

CPSIA information can be obtained
at www.ICGtesting.com
Printed in the USA
FSOW01n1742100717
35929FS